Stoicisr

Stoic Philosophy and the Art of Resilient Living

Jordan Knight

Table of Contents

An Introduction to Stoicism........................ 4

Chapter 1: The Stoics................................... 6

Chapter 2: The Dichotomy of Control.........12

Chapter 3: Pursuit of Virtue....................... 15

Chapter 4: Inner Fortress........................... 18

Chapter 5: Cosmopolitanism......................21

Chapter 6: Emotions and Desires.............. 24

Chapter 7: Endurance of Hardship............ 27

Chapter 8: Reflection and Continuous Learning..30

Chapter 9: Death and Impermanence........ 33

Chapter 10: Universal Reason (Logos).......36

Chapter 11: Detachment............................39

Chapter 12: Quotes from the Stoics............ 42

Conclusion..67

© **Rivercat Books LLC 2023 - All rights reserved.**

The content contained within this book may not be reproduced, duplicated or transmitted without direct written permission from the author or the publisher.

Under no circumstances will any blame or legal responsibility be held against the publisher, or author, for any damages, reparation, or monetary loss due to the information contained within this book, either directly or indirectly.

<u>Legal Notice:</u>

This book is copyright protected. It is only for personal use. You cannot amend, distribute, sell, use, quote or paraphrase any part, or the content within this book, without the consent of the author or publisher.

<u>Disclaimer Notice:</u>

Please note the information contained within this document is for educational and entertainment purposes only. All effort has been executed to present accurate, up to date, reliable, complete information. No warranties of any kind are declared or implied. Readers acknowledge that the author is not engaged in the rendering of legal, financial, medical or professional advice. The content within this book has been derived from various sources. Please consult a licensed professional before attempting any techniques outlined in this book.

By reading this document, the reader agrees that under no circumstances is the author responsible for any losses, direct or indirect, that are incurred as a result of the use of the information contained within this document, including, but not limited to, errors, omissions, or inaccuracies.

An Introduction to Stoicism

Stoicism originated in Athens, Greece, in the early 3rd century BCE. The philosophy was founded by Zeno of Citium, a Phoenician-born merchant who, after suffering a shipwreck, turned to philosophy as a new direction for his life. He began teaching in a public colonnade called the Stoa Poikile, or "Painted Porch," from which the term "Stoicism" was derived. Influenced by the teachings of Socrates, Cynicism, and the early Platonic Academy, Zeno established Stoicism as a comprehensive system of philosophy encompassing ethics, logic, and physics. Stoicism was further developed and refined by subsequent thinkers such as Cleanthes, Chrysippus, and later Roman philosophers like Seneca, Epictetus, and Emperor Marcus Aurelius.

At its core, Stoicism teaches that the path to a good and fulfilling life is found in understanding the natural order of the universe and cultivating personal virtues.

The central tenet of Stoicism revolves around the Dichotomy of Control: recognizing what is within our control and what isn't. According to the Stoics, our reactions, judgments, desires, and emotions are within our control, while external events, the opinions of others, and outcomes are often beyond it. By focusing on improving ourselves and our reactions rather than trying to control the uncontrollable, we can achieve tranquility and peace of mind.

Stoics believe in the rational order of the cosmos, often referred to as the Logos. Everything in the universe, they argue, follows a rational and predictable order. Thus, understanding and accepting this order, rather than resisting or lamenting it, is key to leading a harmonious life. This acceptance extends to hardships, losses, and even death, all of which are viewed as natural parts of existence.

Ethics is paramount in Stoicism, with an emphasis on cultivating personal virtues such as wisdom, courage, justice, and temperance. Stoics strive to live according to their inner nature as rational beings, and in harmony with the external nature of the universe. By doing so, they believe one can achieve eudaimonia, a term often translated as "flourishing" or "fulfillment."

Another crucial Stoic principle is Cosmopolitanism, the idea that all humans belong to a single, global community. This belief fosters a sense of mutual respect and understanding, emphasizing our shared human experience over divisive factors like nationality or social status.

Over time, Stoicism has been adopted, adapted, and revived in various forms, influencing numerous cultural and philosophical movements throughout history. Even today, its teachings offer practical guidance for those seeking clarity, resilience, and contentment in an often chaotic world.

Throughout the following chapters, you will be introduced to the great stoics who contributed to the development and popularity of this enduring philosophy. We will also explore the different principles of stoicism in greater depth. This includes those already mentioned, such as the dichotomy of control, but also other less frequently focused on principles of stoicism such as detachment, continuous learning, and death & impermanence. Finally, this book concludes with a chapter full of quotes from famous stoic philosophers, whose enduring wisdom proves to be truly timeless.

Chapter 1: The Stoics

In this chapter, we will introduce you to some of the most famous Stoics who helped to establish, refine, and popularize the philosophy.

Zeno of Citium

Zeno of Citium (c. 334 – 262 BCE) was an ancient philosopher from the Hellenistic city of Citium in Cyprus. He is best known as the founder of Stoicism. Legend has it that after being shipwrecked in Athens and losing all his possessions, Zeno came across a bookstore where he started reading about Socrates. This encounter ignited his interest in philosophy, leading him to study under various philosophers, including the Cynic Crates of Thebes.

Zeno's teachings, which he began to deliver at the Stoa Poikile (the "Painted Porch") in Athens, laid the foundation for Stoicism. This location of his lectures is what ultimately gave Stoicism its name. Zeno's philosophy emphasized rationality and the acceptance of Fate. He posited that the universe is ordered by a divine rational principle (Logos) and that by aligning one's life with this rationality, one could achieve a state of eudaimonia or flourishing. Central to his teachings was the belief in focusing on what is within our control and accepting what is not.

While many of Zeno's original works have been lost over time, his ideas were further developed and codified by later Stoic thinkers such as Cleanthes and Chrysippus. Through their efforts, and those of Roman Stoics like Seneca, Epictetus, and Marcus Aurelius, Zeno's foundational thoughts on Stoicism proliferated throughout the Greco-Roman world, leaving a lasting impact that resonates even in contemporary philosophy and self-help circles.

Cleanthes

Cleanthes (c. 330 – 230 BCE) was an ancient philosopher from Assos in Asia Minor who became the second head of the Stoic school in Athens, succeeding its founder, Zeno of Citium. Born into modest circumstances, Cleanthes came to Athens with little means and is said to have supported himself initially as a water-carrier, earning him the nickname "the Water-carrier." Despite his financial challenges, Cleanthes was deeply committed to philosophy and became an ardent student of Zeno's teachings.

Assuming leadership of the Stoic school after Zeno's death, Cleanthes played a pivotal role in both preserving and further developing Stoic philosophy. He emphasized the importance of living in accordance with nature and the divine order of the universe, a core tenet of Stoicism. While many of his works have unfortunately been lost, his "Hymn to Zeus" remains, offering valuable insight into his devout perspective on the universe's rational and divine order.

Under Cleanthes' guidance, the Stoic school continued to flourish, paving the way for the next significant Stoic philosopher, Chrysippus, who further systematized and expanded upon the Stoic doctrine. Cleanthes' dedication to Stoic teachings and his role in their early proliferation solidified his place as a foundational figure in the Stoic tradition.

Chrysippus

Chrysippus (c. 279 – 206 BCE) was an ancient philosopher from Soli in Cilicia and is often considered the second founder of Stoicism due to his significant contributions to the school. Following Cleanthes, Chrysippus became the third head of the Stoic school in Athens. Renowned for his prodigious intellectual output, it's said that he wrote over 700 works, although sadly, only fragments of these writings survive today.

Chrysippus' life, while not extensively documented in terms of personal details, was primarily dedicated to philosophy. He was known for his sharp intellect and played a crucial role in the development of the Stoic system, particularly in the areas of logic and ethics. Chrysippus further elaborated on the Stoic doctrines introduced by Zeno and Cleanthes, refining and systematizing them in ways that made Stoicism a more cohesive and comprehensive philosophical system. His work on Stoic logic, for instance, was groundbreaking and formed a central part of the Hellenistic philosophical curriculum.

Without Chrysippus' meticulous and expansive work, Stoicism might not have achieved the lasting impact and coherence it eventually did. His efforts ensured that Stoicism remained a major philosophical force in the Greco-Roman world, influencing countless individuals, including prominent Roman figures like Seneca, Epictetus, and Emperor Marcus Aurelius. Thus, while Zeno laid the foundational stones of Stoicism, it was Chrysippus who constructed much of the intellectual edifice upon them.

Seneca the Younger

Seneca the Younger (c. 4 BCE – 65 CE), often simply referred to as Seneca, was a Roman Stoic philosopher, statesman, and playwright. Born in Corduba (present-day Córdoba, Spain), he was raised in Rome and quickly became immersed in the political and intellectual life of the Roman Empire. Seneca faced various challenges throughout his life, including exile to Corsica due to alleged involvement in an adultery scandal, and a complex relationship with the Emperor Nero, whom he tutored and later served as an advisor.

Seneca's writings on Stoicism stand as some of the most accessible and influential works on the subject. His essays, letters, and dialogues are less technical than some earlier Stoic works, making them more approachable to a broader audience. Through writings such as "Letters to Lucilius," a collection of moral epistles, and essays like "On the Shortness of Life" and "On Anger," Seneca explored the practical application of Stoic principles in daily life, offering guidance on facing challenges, moral conduct, and the pursuit of wisdom.

Beyond philosophy, Seneca also penned tragic plays that resonated with Stoic themes, reflecting the human experience and the challenges of fate and emotion. His influence extended beyond the Stoic community, with his works being read and admired throughout the Roman Empire.

While Seneca did not "create" Stoicism, he played a pivotal role in its adaptation and proliferation within Roman society. His philosophical writings, combined with his high political standing, ensured that Stoic ideas remained influential throughout Rome's elite circles and beyond, bridging the gap between Hellenistic Stoicism and its Roman adaptation.

Epictetus

Epictetus (c. 50 – 135 CE) was an influential Stoic philosopher born into slavery in Hierapolis, Phrygia (present-day Turkey). He spent much of his early life in Rome as a slave to Epaphroditos, an administrative secretary to Emperor Nero. During this period, despite his status, he was permitted to study philosophy under the Stoic teacher Musonius Rufus. Eventually gaining his freedom, Epictetus began teaching philosophy in Rome, and after the expulsion of philosophers by Emperor Domitian, he relocated to Nicopolis in Greece, where he established a prominent school.

Epictetus' Stoicism centers around the notion of control. He posited that while individuals cannot control external events, they can control their reactions and judgments. This dichotomy of control, as it's often called, is a defining feature of his teachings. Unlike many of his contemporaries, Epictetus wrote nothing himself. Instead, his teachings were meticulously recorded by his student Arrian, the most notable of which are the "Enchiridion" (Handbook) and the "Discourses." These works emphasize the practical application of Stoicism in daily life, guiding readers on how to lead a virtuous life and achieve inner peace by aligning their will with nature and focusing on what is truly within their control.

Epictetus' influence on Stoicism and Western philosophy at large is profound. His writings, especially the "Enchiridion," became essential reading for those interested in Stoic philosophy, serving as a practical guide to Stoic ethics. His teachings not only continued the tradition of Stoicism in the Roman era but also influenced later philosophical and religious thinkers, cementing his legacy as one of the great Stoic philosophers.

Marcus Aurelius

Marcus Aurelius (121 – 180 CE) was Roman Emperor from 161 to 180 CE and is often remembered as the last of the "Five Good Emperors." Born into an aristocratic family in Rome, Marcus Aurelius was adopted by Emperor Antoninus Pius, whom he succeeded as emperor. His reign was marked by military conflicts in various parts of the Roman Empire, including campaigns against the Parthians and Germanic tribes, as well as dealing with internal revolts and the outbreak of the Antonine Plague. Beyond his political and military endeavors, Marcus Aurelius is celebrated for his deep commitment to Stoic philosophy. He is arguably the most famous Stoic philosopher-emperor and his work, "Meditations," offers an intimate glimpse into his Stoic beliefs and practices. Written primarily as personal notes and reflections during his military campaigns, "Meditations" delves into themes of resilience, duty, death, and the transient nature of life, all underpinned by Stoic principles. Unlike other Stoic writings that present a systematic exploration of the philosophy, Marcus's work is introspective and serves as a testament to his attempt to internalize and live by Stoic virtues amidst the challenges of ruling an empire.

Marcus Aurelius did not contribute to the creation or foundational advancement of Stoicism in the way earlier figures like Zeno, Chrysippus, or even Seneca did. However, his role in the proliferation of Stoicism is invaluable. As both an emperor and a philosopher, he exemplified the practical application of Stoic ideals in a position of immense power. His "Meditations" has been continuously read and revered since antiquity, influencing countless individuals across various disciplines and eras, making him a central figure in the Stoic tradition and its enduring legacy.

Chapter 2: The Dichotomy of Control

The Dichotomy of Control is a foundational principle in Stoic philosophy, centering on the idea that some things are within our control, while others are not. By recognizing and internalizing this division, individuals can cultivate a sense of equanimity and resilience in the face of life's challenges.

The concept is most famously articulated by the Stoic philosopher Epictetus in his works, particularly in the "Enchiridion" (Handbook) and the "Discourses." While the notion of focusing on what's within one's power can be found in earlier Stoic works, it's Epictetus who crystallizes it into a clear, actionable principle.

The Dichotomy of Control essentially breaks down into two categories:

1) **Things Within Our Control:** This includes our judgments, desires, aversions, and, in general, whatever is of our own doing. Our attitudes, reactions, decisions, and internal beliefs are primary examples.

2) **Things Outside Our Control:** This encompasses practically everything else, including the behavior of other people, external events, our reputation, and the inevitable course of nature or fate.

Recognizing and adhering to the Dichotomy of Control offers several benefits:

1) **Reduced Anxiety:** By accepting that many things in life are beyond our influence, we can relieve the anxieties and frustrations that arise from trying to control the uncontrollable.

2) **Improved Resilience:** When adversities strike, understanding this dichotomy allows us to redirect our energy towards constructive responses rather than lamenting circumstances.

3) **Enhanced Decision-Making:** It provides clarity in situations, helping us focus on actionable aspects rather than getting mired in externalities.

4) **Inner Peace:** By aligning our concerns with what's truly in our control, we can cultivate a more profound sense of inner peace and contentment.

To apply the Dichotomy of Control in daily life:

1) **Reflect Before Reacting:** When faced with challenges, pause to discern what aspects are within your control.

2) **Adjust Expectations:** Set goals based on your actions and attitudes rather than external outcomes.

3) **Acceptance:** Embrace external events as they come, understanding that lamenting or resisting them is often futile and mentally exhausting.

4) **Focus on Effort:** Concentrate on your effort and intention, which you can control, rather than the results, which often you cannot.

In essence, the Stoic Dichotomy of Control serves as a guiding compass, steering us towards a more centered, purposeful, and tranquil existence, regardless of external circumstances.

Chapter 3: Pursuit of Virtue

The Pursuit of Virtue is a central tenet in Stoic philosophy, emphasizing the role of virtue as the highest good and the foundation for a fulfilling life. For the Stoics, a life guided by virtue is the surest path to eudaimonia, or a flourishing existence.

The emphasis on virtue can be traced back to the early days of Stoic philosophy with its founder, Zeno of Citium. While Stoicism wasn't the only ancient philosophy to prioritize virtue (it played a significant role in Socratic, Platonic, and Aristotelian thought as well), the Stoics gave it a distinct centrality and definition in their ethical system.

The core tenets of the Pursuit of Virtue are as follows:

1) **Virtue as the Highest Good:** For Stoics, virtues are intrinsic goods, and all other things (wealth, reputation, health) are indifferent in terms of leading a good life. While these "indifferents" can be preferred or dispreferred, they neither contribute to nor detract from one's virtue.

2) **Four Cardinal Virtues:** Stoicism identifies four primary virtues:

1. Wisdom (the ability to judge correctly and to distinguish the true from the false)

2. Courage (facing challenges and difficulties with integrity)

3. Justice (treating others with fairness and kindness)

4. Temperance (self-control and moderation in all aspects of life)

3) **Rationality and Nature:** Virtue is tied to living according to nature and reason. For the Stoics, to live virtuously is to live in alignment with rational nature, both our own and that of the universe.

The benefits of this principle of Stoicism can be described as:

1) **Genuine Fulfillment:** By prioritizing virtue, one finds a deeper, more enduring sense of fulfillment than transient pleasures or external validations can offer.

2) **Moral Clarity:** A focus on virtue provides clear moral guidance, helping individuals navigate complex ethical situations.

3) **Resilience:** Virtuous living promotes resilience, as one's sense of self-worth and purpose is anchored in

internal values rather than fluctuating external circumstances.

4) **Harmony with Nature:** By aligning oneself with nature and reason, one experiences a profound sense of harmony and connection with the world.

To apply the principle of the Pursuit of Virtue in daily life:

1) **Reflect on Actions:** Regularly evaluate your actions and intentions, asking whether they align with the cardinal virtues.

2) **Educate Oneself:** Engage with philosophical and ethical texts or discussions that enhance understanding and appreciation of virtue.

3) **Practice:** Actively seek out opportunities in daily life to practice virtues, be it showing courage in the face of adversity or exercising temperance in moments of excess.

4) **Mindfulness:** Cultivate mindfulness to ensure that decisions and reactions are based on reasoned judgment rather than impulsive emotions.

In summary, the Pursuit of Virtue in Stoicism is the heart of its ethical framework. It provides a sturdy foundation for individuals to lead meaningful, purposeful lives, grounded in moral integrity and aligned with the rational order of nature.

Chapter 4: Inner Fortress

The Inner Fortress is a metaphorical concept in Stoic philosophy that represents the idea of an impenetrable inner sanctum of the mind, where one can find refuge and maintain tranquility regardless of external circumstances.

The notion of the Inner Fortress is most famously associated with Marcus Aurelius, the Roman Emperor and Stoic philosopher. His work, "Meditations," offers numerous reflections that allude to the idea of an internal citadel or refuge, where the Stoic practitioner can retreat to remain unaffected by external adversities.

The core tenets of this Stoic concept are as follows:

1) **Inner Autonomy:** The Inner Fortress emphasizes the idea that, while we might not control external events, we have complete dominion over our internal responses and judgments.

2) **Mental Refuge:** This internal citadel serves as a mental space of refuge, where the Stoic can remain serene and undisturbed, regardless of external chaos or adversity.

3) **Distinction Between Internal and External:** The Inner Fortress embodies the Stoic Dichotomy of Control, which distinguishes between things we can control (our thoughts, judgments, reactions) and those we can't (external events, opinions of others).

4) **Imperviousness to Harm:** Inside this fortress, the individual remains invulnerable to external harms, not because harms don't occur, but because they don't penetrate the inner sanctum of reasoned judgment and virtuous disposition.

The benefits of Inner Fortress are:

1) **Resilience:** The Inner Fortress provides a foundation for resilience, allowing individuals to navigate challenges without being emotionally overwhelmed.

2) **Consistent Tranquility:** It offers a consistent state of inner peace and tranquility, regardless of external conditions.

3) **Clarity of Mind:** By retreating to this internal space, individuals can gain clarity and perspective, free from the immediate pressures of the outside world.

4) **Emotional Independence:** It promotes emotional independence, detaching one's sense of well-being from external validations or circumstances.

To cultivate and maintain the Inner Fortress, practice the following:

1) **Daily Reflection:** Engage in daily philosophical reflection, reminding oneself of the distinction between the internal and external.

2) **Mindfulness Practices:** Use mindfulness or meditative practices to center oneself and create a clear mental space.

3) **Challenge Reactions:** When faced with adversity, challenge immediate emotional reactions by retreating to the Inner Fortress and asking if the perceived harm truly affects one's inner virtue or if it's merely an external event.

4) **Study and Contemplation:** Regularly engage with Stoic writings and teachings to strengthen and fortify the foundations of this inner citadel.

In essence, the Inner Fortress represents the Stoic ideal of achieving an unassailable state of inner peace and virtue. It's the embodiment of the belief that, with rigorous practice and reflection, one can remain steadfast and serene amidst the inevitable storms of life.

Chapter 5: Cosmopolitanism

Cosmopolitanism is a significant principle in Stoic philosophy that advocates the idea that all human beings are members of a single, universal family and that our primary allegiance is to this global community rather than to our local, parochial affiliations.

The roots of cosmopolitanism can be found in early Greek philosophical thought, but it was the Stoics who developed and integrated it fully into their ethical framework. Notably, the Cynic philosopher Diogenes of Sinope is credited with stating that he was a "citizen of the world" (cosmopolites in Greek), but it was the Stoics, especially the Roman Stoics like Seneca, Epictetus, and Marcus Aurelius, who fleshed out the idea and connected it with their broader philosophical worldview.

The core tenets of Cosmopolitanism are as follows:

1) **Universal Brotherhood:** At the heart of Stoic cosmopolitanism is the belief in the universal brotherhood of humankind. All humans, according to the Stoics, share in the divine logos or rational principle, which binds us together in a cosmic fraternity.

2) **Transcending Parochialism:** Stoics believed in transcending local loyalties and identities, be they of city, tribe, or nation. Instead, their allegiance was to humanity as a whole.

3) **Moral Obligation:** With this universal perspective comes a moral obligation: to treat all individuals justly and kindly, regardless of their background or status.

The benefits of Cosmopolitanism include:

1) **Universal Morality:** Cosmopolitanism promotes a moral code that is universal and based on human dignity rather than contingent on local customs or laws.

2) **Tolerance and Understanding:** It fosters tolerance and understanding between different peoples and cultures.

3) **Unified Perspective:** By viewing humanity as a single entity, one gains a broader perspective that can be beneficial in understanding global challenges and solutions.

4) **Reduction of Conflict:** Emphasizing shared human values can help reduce conflicts based on parochial interests or identities.

To apply the principle of Cosmopolitanism in daily life:

1) **Cultivate Empathy:** Strive to understand and empathize with people from diverse backgrounds and cultures.

2) **Broaden Your Horizons:** Seek out literature, arts, and experiences from around the world.

3) **Engage in Dialogue:** Engage in constructive dialogue with individuals from different backgrounds, aiming for mutual understanding.

4) **Promote Unity:** Actively work towards causes that promote global unity, understanding, and cooperation.

In summary, Cosmopolitanism in Stoic philosophy embodies the belief that humanity is interconnected, and our shared rational nature binds us in a moral community. This perspective encourages mutual respect, understanding, and cooperation among the diverse members of the human family.

Chapter 6: Emotions and Desires

Emotions and Desires play a pivotal role in Stoic philosophy, emphasizing rational judgment over impulsive reactions and understanding that unchecked desires lead to suffering. Stoicism provides tools for managing and understanding these internal experiences.

While the broader ideas about human emotions and desires can be found in the foundational teachings of early Stoics like Zeno of Citium, the concepts were deeply expanded upon and made more accessible by later Stoics. Seneca, Epictetus, and Marcus Aurelius, for instance, provided many reflections and guidance on handling emotions and desires in their writings.

The core tenets of dealing with Emotions and Desires according to Stoicism are as follows:

1) **Nature of Emotions:** Stoics believed that emotions aren't inherently bad but become problematic when they're irrational or unchecked. They stem from our beliefs and judgments, not from external events themselves.

2) **Desires and Aversions:** Stoicism teaches that suffering often arises from unmet desires or from experiencing things we want to avoid. The goal isn't to suppress desires but to align them with nature and reason.

3) **Judgments Over Reactions:** Stoics maintain that it's not external events but our judgments about them that cause emotional reactions. By examining and correcting these judgments, we can achieve tranquility.

4) **Distinction of Control:** A key aspect of managing emotions and desires is understanding the Stoic dichotomy of control — recognizing what is within our control (our judgments, intentions, reactions) and what is not (external events, opinions of others).

The benefits of adopting a Stoic approach to Emotions and Desires include:

1) **Inner Tranquility:** By understanding and managing emotions and desires, one can achieve a state of inner peace or "ataraxia," undisturbed by external events.

2) **Resilience:** Developing a stoic attitude toward emotions and desires equips individuals with resilience, allowing them to face adversities with a balanced mind.

3) **Clearer Decision Making:** Without being overwhelmed or blinded by strong emotions and desires, decisions become more rational and aligned with one's true values.

4) **Enhanced Relationships:** By not being slaves to impulsive reactions, individuals can foster better, more understanding relationships with others.

To incorporate the Stoic view on Emotions and Desires:

1) **Reflect and Analyze:** When strong emotions arise, pause to reflect on the judgments causing them. Ask whether the judgment is accurate or based on an irrational belief.

2) **Manage Expectations:** Understand that many desires, especially when they concern external outcomes, can lead to disappointment. Align desires with personal virtue and effort instead.

3) **Practice Premeditation:** Engage in "premeditatio malorum," where you visualize potential challenges or negative events. This prepares the mind and reduces impulsive emotional reactions.

4) **Mindfulness and Awareness:** Develop a daily practice of mindfulness to become more aware of arising emotions and desires before they take control.

In summation, the Stoic principle regarding Emotions and Desires emphasizes mastery over one's internal life. By understanding the nature of our emotional responses and desires and aligning them with reason and nature, one can navigate life with equanimity and purpose.

Chapter 7: Endurance of Hardship

Endurance of Hardship is a fundamental aspect of Stoic philosophy, emphasizing the capacity to withstand and grow from life's adversities. It's not merely about passive acceptance, but about actively using challenges as opportunities for growth and enlightenment.

The notion of enduring hardship with grace can be traced back to the very origins of Stoicism. Early Stoics, like Zeno of Citium and Chrysippus, laid the foundational ideas. However, the most poignant insights and real-life demonstrations come from figures like Epictetus, a former slave who became a renowned philosopher, Seneca, who faced political intrigues and exile, and Marcus Aurelius, the Roman Emperor who wrote his Meditations during military campaigns and the challenges of leadership.

The core tenets of Endurance of Hardship are as follows:

1) **Value of Adversity:** Stoics see hardships not as mere misfortunes but as opportunities for growth, moral refinement, and gaining wisdom.

2) **Training and Preparation:** Life's adversities are likened to athletic training; they strengthen the soul just as exercise strengthens the body.

3) **The Dichotomy of Control:** Recognizing what is and isn't within our control allows us to focus our

energies rightly. We might not control events, but we control our response.

4) **Temporary Nature of Life:** Stoics frequently reflect on the impermanence of life, helping them maintain perspective during tough times.

The benefits of embracing a Stoic approach to the Endurance of Hardship include:

1) **Resilience:** By viewing hardships as natural and transformative, Stoics develop a robustness that helps them rebound from life's blows.

2) **Emotional Equilibrium:** Stoics cultivate a stable emotional state, undeterred by external misfortunes.

3) **Clear Perspective:** By seeing the larger picture and the transient nature of life, Stoics prevent momentary hardships from overwhelming them.

4) **Growth and Wisdom:** Hardships, when approached Stoically, lead to personal growth, increased wisdom, and moral fortitude.

To embody the Stoic principle of Endurance of Hardship:

1) **Reflect on Impermanence:** Regularly meditate on the temporary nature of life, known as "memento mori", to gain perspective.

2) **Visualize Challenges:** Engage in "premeditatio malorum," anticipating potential setbacks and mentally preparing for them.

3) **Controlled Exposure:** Deliberately expose oneself to controlled hardships (like cold showers, fasting, etc.) to build mental toughness.

4) **Journaling:** Just as Marcus Aurelius wrote his Meditations, journaling can offer clarity, allowing one to process and learn from adversities.

In essence, the Stoic approach to the Endurance of Hardship reframes adversities as invaluable opportunities. Instead of shying away from challenges, Stoics embrace them, utilizing each one as a stepping stone to a more virtuous, enlightened existence.

Chapter 8: Reflection and Continuous Learning

Reflection and Continuous Learning are vital aspects of Stoic philosophy, underscoring the importance of introspection, self-improvement, and the lifelong journey of acquiring wisdom.

While the core ideas of Stoicism trace back to early Stoic thinkers like Zeno and Chrysippus, the emphasis on reflection and learning is prominently showcased in the writings of later Stoics. Epictetus frequently stressed the importance of self-examination and learning from both experience and study. Seneca's letters are filled with recommendations for study, introspection, and the value of time spent in reflection. Marcus Aurelius's "Meditations" itself is a product of his reflective practice, providing insights into his thoughts and lessons from his daily life.

According to Stoicism, the core tenets of Reflection and Continuous Learning are:

1) **Introspection:** Stoics believed in the regular examination of one's thoughts, actions, and feelings to ensure alignment with virtue and reason.

2) **Lifelong Learning:** Stoicism is not a philosophy to be merely studied but lived. This requires continuous learning and adaptation.

3) **Value of Time:** Stoics, especially Seneca, emphasized the importance of using one's time wisely, dedicating it to meaningful pursuits, including study and reflection.

4) **Learning from Others:** Stoics advocate for learning not just from personal experiences but also from the wisdom of others, both past and present.

The benefits of practicing Reflection and Continuous Learning include:

1) **Personal Growth:** Regular reflection and learning facilitate continuous personal and moral development.

2) **Improved Decision Making:** By continually refining one's understanding and wisdom, one can make better, more informed decisions.

3) **Emotional Stability:** Reflection helps in understanding and managing emotions, leading to a more balanced and tranquil state of mind.

4) **Deepened Understanding:** Continuous learning provides a deeper understanding of oneself, others, and the world at large.

To integrate the Stoic principle of Reflection and Continuous Learning, try the following practices:

1) **Daily Review:** Just as the Stoics did, take time at the beginning or end of each day to reflect on actions, thoughts, and lessons of the day.

2) **Journaling:** Maintain a journal to note reflections, insights, and wisdom acquired.

3) **Seek Wisdom:** Regularly read and study philosophy and other disciplines, drawing lessons that can be applied to daily life.

4) **Engage in Dialogue:** Discuss philosophical and ethical questions with others to gain varied perspectives and insights.

5) **Time Management:** Recognize the value of time and ensure that a good portion is dedicated to introspective and educational activities.

In a nutshell, the Stoic principle of Reflection and Continuous Learning accentuates the unending journey of self-improvement and the pursuit of wisdom. Stoicism reminds us that life's true purpose isn't merely to live but to live well, and this is facilitated through continuous introspection and growth.

Chapter 9: Death and Impermanence

Death and Impermanence is a cornerstone of Stoic philosophy, emphasizing the transient nature of life and all things within it. By contemplating and accepting the inevitability of death and the impermanence of experiences, Stoics cultivate a deeper appreciation for life and develop resilience against the fear of loss.

Reflection on death and life's impermanence permeates the teachings of many Stoic philosophers. While the early founders of Stoicism like Zeno and Chrysippus would have introduced these ideas, they were profoundly elaborated upon by later Stoics. Marcus Aurelius wrote extensively on the transient nature of life in his "Meditations." Seneca's letters and essays, especially "On the Shortness of Life," also explore this theme. Epictetus too discussed the fleeting nature of life and the need to be prepared for death.

The core tenets of Death and Impermanence are:

1) **Memento Mori:** This Latin phrase, meaning "remember you must die," encapsulates the Stoic practice of regularly reflecting on one's mortality to imbue life with purpose and urgency.

2) **Nature's Course:** Death is seen as a natural and inevitable part of life, not something to be feared.

3) **Transient Pleasures and Sorrows:** Both positive and negative experiences are fleeting, so Stoics learn not to become overly attached or aversive.

4) **Value of the Present:** With the recognition of life's brevity, Stoics emphasize the importance of living fully in the present moment.

The benefits of adopting a Stoic approach to Death and Impermanence include:

1) **Heightened Appreciation:** Reflecting on impermanence leads to a deeper appreciation of life's moments, both big and small.

2) **Resilience:** Understanding and accepting the transient nature of life reduces the fear of loss and the anguish of death.

3) **Purposeful Living:** Contemplation of death provides clarity on life's priorities, urging one to live purposefully and virtuously.

4) **Emotional Balance:** Recognizing the fleeting nature of emotions and experiences helps maintain equanimity in the face of life's ups and downs.

To adopt the Stoic principle of Death and Impermanence, practice the following:

1) **Regular Reflection:** Dedicate time to meditate on the temporary nature of life, personal experiences, and the inevitability of death.

2) **Engage with Literature:** Read texts, both Stoic and non-Stoic, that delve into themes of death and impermanence.

3) **Practice Gratitude:** Daily gratitude practices can help in appreciating the present and the transient gifts of life.

4) **Limit Attachment:** Recognize the temporary nature of possessions, status, and even relationships, and practice non-attachment.

5) **Live Deliberately:** With the acknowledgment of life's brevity, ensure that actions align with one's values and virtues.

In essence, the Stoic principle of Death and Impermanence serves as a potent reminder of life's fleeting nature. Instead of inducing fear or sadness, this realization encourages Stoics to live fully, virtuously, and with deep appreciation for every moment.

Chapter 10: Universal Reason (Logos)

Universal Reason (Logos) is an integral concept within Stoic philosophy, representing the rational principle that governs the universe. This idea of a universal, divine reason is akin to the ancient notion of a cosmic order or natural law that oversees all existence.

The idea of the Logos did not originate with the Stoics but has roots in earlier philosophical traditions, notably with Heraclitus, who posited that a governing principle or "Logos" underpins the universe's order. The Stoics, beginning with the school's founder Zeno of Citium and further developed by Chrysippus, adopted and refined this concept, embedding it within their philosophy as a foundational tenet.

The core tenets of the Logos are as follows:

1) **Cosmic Rationality:** The Stoics believed that the universe is not chaotic but is ordered by the Logos, a rational and divine principle.

2) **Human Rationality:** Humans, being part of the universe, have a share of this Logos in the form of rational faculties. This connection to the divine grants humans a unique position within nature.

3) **Nature's Alignment:** Living according to nature, a crucial Stoic maxim, means aligning one's life with this universal reason or Logos.

4) **Determinism:** Many Stoics, recognizing the Logos's governing nature, held a deterministic view of the universe, believing that everything unfolds according to this divine reason.

The benefits of adopting the Stoic principle of Universal Reason (Logos) include:

1) **Sense of Order:** Belief in the Logos provides a framework through which life's challenges can be seen as part of a greater, comprehensible order, reducing feelings of chaos or randomness.

2) **Guided Morality:** Understanding that humans share in the Logos offers a foundation for moral and ethical behavior, as one is acting in harmony with the universe's rational principle.

3) **Inner Peace:** Recognizing and accepting the unfolding of events as part of the Logos can foster tranquility, even in the face of adversity.

4) **Purpose and Connection:** Belief in the Logos imparts a sense of connectedness to a greater whole and a deeper understanding of one's role in the universe.

To embrace the Stoic principle of Universal Reason (Logos), practice the following:

1) **Philosophical Study:** Delve into Stoic texts and writings to gain a comprehensive understanding of the Logos concept and its implications.

2) **Meditation:** Engage in meditative practices that reflect on the universe's order and one's place within it.

3) **Act Rationally:** Strive to make decisions based on reason and logic, embodying the rational principle believed to govern the cosmos.

4) **Acceptance Practice:** Cultivate acceptance of life events, viewing them as unfolding according to a greater cosmic order.

5) **Ethical Living:** Recognize the shared rationality among all humans, fostering a sense of kinship and encouraging ethical actions towards others.

In summary, the Stoic principle of Universal Reason (Logos) posits a universe governed by rationality and order. By recognizing and aligning with this cosmic reason, Stoics seek to live lives of purpose, meaning, and virtue, harmoniously intertwined with the universe's broader fabric.

Chapter 11: Detachment

Detachment in Stoic philosophy refers to the intentional practice of not letting oneself be excessively affected by external events, possessions, or the opinions of others. It doesn't mean suppressing emotions or evading life's responsibilities but rather approaching life with a calm and balanced perspective that allows for inner peace regardless of external circumstances.

The concept of detachment finds its roots in the foundational teachings of Stoicism, from the early musings of Zeno of Citium to the refined thoughts of Epictetus, Seneca, and Marcus Aurelius. While not attributed to a single inventor, Epictetus, in particular, emphasized detachment as essential to achieving tranquility, especially in his famous distinction between things within our control and things outside of it.

The core tenets of Detachment are as follows:

1) **Control and Acceptance:** Recognize the dichotomy of control. Some things are up to us, while others are not. Accepting this distinction aids in detaching from outcomes.

2) **Transient Nature of Life:** Understand and internalize the temporary nature of all things, which makes it easier to remain detached from them.

3) **Value Internal Over External:** Prioritize internal virtues and character over external achievements or validations.

4) **Freedom from Passions:** By mastering desires and practicing restraint, one can attain apatheia, or freedom from harmful passions.

The benefits of adopting the Stoic principle of Detachment include:

1) **Inner Peace:** Detachment allows one to maintain a sense of calm and serenity regardless of external chaos or pressures.

2) **Resilience:** By not being overly attached to outcomes, individuals can more easily bounce back from setbacks.

3) **Clear Judgment:** A detached perspective enables more objective and rational decision-making.

4) **Reduced Suffering:** Understanding and accepting the impermanence of life reduces the anguish of loss or unmet expectations.

To adopt the Stoic principle of Detachment, practice the following:

1) **Mindful Awareness:** Regularly assess where you might be overly attached or reactive and recalibrate accordingly.

2) **Practice Dispassion:** When faced with strong desires or aversions, pause and question the underlying beliefs or assumptions.

3) **Reflect on Impermanence:** Regularly contemplate the transient nature of life, possessions, and relationships.

4) **Engage in Negative Visualization:** This Stoic exercise involves imagining the loss of things or people one values, not to induce sadness but to appreciate them more and strengthen detachment.

5) **Value Inner Virtues:** Consistently remind oneself of the importance of inner virtues over external rewards or recognitions.

In essence, the Stoic principle of Detachment encourages individuals to engage fully with life while maintaining a balanced perspective that protects inner peace. By distinguishing between what we can control and what we cannot, and by valuing internal virtues above external accolades, Stoicism offers a path to a life of contentment, resilience, and meaningful purpose.

Chapter 12: Quotes from the Stoics

In this final chapter, you will find a range of quotes from some of the famous Stoic philosophers. You may wish to read through these all at once, read a quote or two each day, or simply return to this chapter whenever you are seeking some wisdom. Although the Stoics quoted here lived thousands of years ago, the timeless wisdom within their words is just as applicable today as it was back then.

"Our life is what our thoughts make it."

Marcus Aurelius

"The best revenge is not to be like your enemy."

Marcus Aurelius

"Man is not worried by real problems so much as by his imagined anxieties about real problems."

Epictetus

"It is not death that a man should fear, but he should fear never beginning to live."

Marcus Aurelius

"He who fears death will never do anything worth of a man who is alive."

Seneca

"If you wish to be loved, love."

Seneca

"Don't explain your philosophy. Embody it."

Epictetus

"You have power over your mind – not outside events. Realize this, and you will find strength."

Marcus Aurelius

"The obstacle is the way."

Marcus Aurelius

"We suffer more in imagination than in reality."

Seneca

"All external events are beyond our control; we should accept calmly and dispassionately whatever happens."

Epictetus

"It's not what happens to you, but how you react to it that matters."

Epictetus

"The key is to keep company only with people who uplift you, whose presence calls forth your best."

Epictetus

"Difficulties strengthen the mind, as labor does the body."

Seneca

"The universe is change; our life is what our thoughts make it."

Marcus Aurelius

"We should always be asking ourselves: 'Is this something that is, or is not, in my control?'"

Epictetus

"People hide their truest nature. I understood that; I even applauded it. What sort of world would it be if people bled all over the sidewalks, if they wept under trees, smacked whomever they despised, kissed strangers, revealed themselves?"

Marcus Aurelius

"Sometimes even to live is an act of courage."

Seneca

"Waste no more time arguing about what a good man should be. Be one."

Marcus Aurelius

"The first step: Don't be anxious. Nature controls it all."

Marcus Aurelius

"He who laughs at himself never runs out of things to laugh at."

Epictetus

"Only the educated are free."

Epictetus

"Life is neither good or evil, but only a place for good and evil."

Marcus Aurelius

"Fate leads the willing and drags along the reluctant."

Seneca

"It is not because things are difficult that we do not dare; it is because we do not dare that they are difficult."

Seneca

"No great thing is created suddenly."

Epictetus

"We are more often frightened than hurt, and we suffer more from imagination than from reality."

Seneca

"Death is a release from the impressions of the senses, and from desires that make us their puppets, and from the vagaries of the mind, and from the hard service of the flesh."

Marcus Aurelius

"If you really want to escape the things that harass you, what you're needing is not to be in a different place but to be a different person."

Seneca

"To accuse others for one's own misfortunes is a sign of want of education. To accuse oneself shows that one's education has begun. To accuse neither oneself nor others shows that one's education is complete."

Epictetus

"While we wait for life, life passes."

Seneca

"To be everywhere is to be nowhere."

Seneca

"If you seek truth, you will not seek victory by dishonorable means, and if you find truth you will become invincible."

Epictetus

"When you are offended at any man's fault, turn to yourself and study your own failings. Then you will forget your anger."

Epictetus

"Time is a sort of river of passing events, and strong is its current; no sooner is a thing brought to sight than it is swept by and another takes its place, and this too will be swept away."

Marcus Aurelius

"Begin at once to live, and count each separate day as a separate life."

Seneca

"First say to yourself what you would be; and then do what you have to do."

Epictetus

"If you want to improve, be content to be thought foolish and stupid."

Epictetus

"The good or ill of a man lies within his own will."

Epictetus

"Let us prepare our minds as if we'd come to the very end of life. Let us postpone nothing. Let us balance life's books each day... The one who puts the finishing touches on their life each day is never short of time."

Seneca

"How long are you going to wait before you demand the best for yourself and in no instance bypass the discriminations of reason? You have been given the principles that you ought to endorse, and you have endorsed them. What kind of teacher, then, are you still waiting for in order to refer your self-improvement to him?"

Epictetus

"There is a time for departure even when there's no certain place to go."

Seneca

"Cling tooth and nail to the following rule: Not to give in to adversity, never to trust prosperity, and always take full note of fortune's habit of behaving just as she pleases, treating her as if she were actually going to do everything it is in her power to do."

Seneca

"Whenever you are about to find fault with someone, ask yourself the following question: What fault of mine most nearly resembles the one I am about to criticize?"

Marcus Aurelius

"Associate with people who are likely to improve you."

Seneca

"He who is brave is free."

Seneca

"All things fade into the storied past, and in a little while are shrouded in oblivion. Even to men whose lives were a blaze of glory this comes to pass; as to the rest, the breath is hardly out of them before, in Homer's words, they are 'lost to sight alike and hearsay'."

Marcus Aurelius

"I begin to speak only when I'm certain what I'll say isn't better left unsaid."

Cato

"To be even-minded is the greatest virtue."

Heraclitus

"It is in your power to withdraw yourself whenever you desire. Perfect tranquility within consists in the good ordering of the mind, the realm of your own."

Marcus Aurelius

"The more we value things outside our control, the less control we have."

Epictetus

"The world turns aside to let any man pass who knows where he is going."

Epictetus

"It does not matter what you bear, but how you bear it."

Seneca

"Everything we hear is an opinion, not a fact. Everything we see is a perspective, not the truth."

Marcus Aurelius

"Don't seek to have events happen as you wish, but wish them to happen as they do happen, and all will be well with you."

Epictetus

"Apply yourself both now and in the next life. Without effort, you cannot be prosperous. Though the land be good, you cannot have an abundant crop without cultivation."

Plato

"If it is not right, do not do it, if it is not true, do not say it."

Marcus Aurelius

"The art of living is more like wrestling than dancing."

Marcus Aurelius

"If you would be a reader, read; if a writer, write."

Epictetus

"Circumstances don't make the man, they only reveal him to himself."

Epictetus

"If you accomplish something good with hard work, the labor passes quickly, but the good endures; if you do something shameful in pursuit of pleasure, the pleasure passes quickly, but the shame endures."

Musonius Rufus

"It is impossible for a man to learn what he thinks he already knows."

Epictetus

"If someone succeeds in provoking you, realize that your mind is complicit in the provocation."

Epictetus

"Whatever happens to you has been waiting to happen since the beginning of time."

Marcus Aurelius

"If a person gave your body to any stranger he met on his way, you would certainly be angry. And do you feel no shame in handing over your own mind to be confused and mystified by anyone who happens to verbally attack you?"

Epictetus

"If you are distressed by anything external, the pain is not due to the thing itself, but to your estimate of it; and this you have the power to revoke at any moment."

Marcus Aurelius

"The whole future lies in uncertainty: live immediately."

Seneca

"For it is not death or pain that is to be feared, but the fear of pain or death."

Epictetus

"What upsets people is not things themselves but their judgments about these things."

Epictetus

"Freedom is the only worthy goal in life. It is won by disregarding things that lie beyond our control."

Epictetus

"The happiness of your life depends upon the quality of your thoughts."

Marcus Aurelius

"You always own the option of having no opinion. There is never any need to get worked up or to trouble your soul about things you can't control. These things are not asking to be judged by you. Leave them alone."

Marcus Aurelius

"First learn the meaning of what you say, and then speak."

Epictetus

"You act like mortals in all that you fear, and like immortals in all that you desire."

Seneca

"It is the nature of the wise to resist pleasures, but the foolish to be a slave to them."

Epictetus

"The greatest remedy for anger is delay."

Seneca

"It is not the man who has too little, but the man who craves more, that is poor."

Seneca

"Whenever you get an impression of some pleasure, as with any impression, guard yourself from being carried away by it, let it await your action, give yourself a pause. After that, bring to mind both times, first when you have enjoyed the pleasure and later when you will regret it and hate yourself. Then compare to those the joy and satisfaction you'd feel for abstaining altogether."

Epictetus

"The chief task in life is simply this: to identify and separate matters so that I can say clearly to myself which are externals not under my control, and which have to do with the choices I actually control."

Epictetus

"Luck is what happens when preparation meets opportunity."

Seneca

"A gem cannot be polished without friction, nor a man perfected without trials."

Seneca

"People are not disturbed by things, but by the views they take of them."

Epictetus

"The soul becomes dyed with the color of its thoughts."

Marcus Aurelius

"Until we have begun to go without them, we fail to realize how unnecessary many things are. We've been using them not because we needed them but because we had them."

Seneca

"To live happily is an inward power of the soul."

Marcus Aurelius

"Man is affected not by events but by the view he takes of them."

Epictetus

"When another blames you or hates you, or people voice similar criticisms, go to their souls, penetrate inside and see what sort of people they are. You will realize that there is no need to be racked with anxiety that they should hold any particular opinion about you."

Marcus Aurelius

"To be even-minded is the greatest virtue."

Heraclitus

"The bravest sight in the world is to see a great man struggling against adversity."

Seneca

"Events do not just happen, but arrive by appointment."

Epictetus

"Wealth consists not in having great possessions, but in having few wants."

Epictetus

"It is not because things are difficult that we do not dare; it is because we do not dare that they are difficult."

Seneca

"The best way to avenge yourself is to not be like that."

Marcus Aurelius

"The greatest obstacle to living is expectancy, which hangs upon tomorrow and loses today."

Seneca

"Time heals what reason cannot."

Seneca

"When you transform your mind, everything you experience is transformed."

Marcus Aurelius

"We have two ears and one mouth so that we can listen twice as much as we speak."

Epictetus

"Attach yourself to what is spiritually superior, regardless of what other people think or do. Hold to your true aspirations no matter what is going on around you."

Epictetus

"There is only one way to happiness and that is to cease worrying about things which are beyond the power of our will."

Epictetus

"A wise man is content with his lot, whatever it may be, without wishing for what he has not."

Seneca

"What is the point of dragging up sufferings that are over, of being miserable now because you were miserable then?"

Seneca

"True happiness is to understand our duties toward God and man; to enjoy the present, without any anxious dependence on the future."

Seneca

"Life is very short and anxious for those who forget the past, neglect the present, and fear the future."

Seneca

"There is no easy way from the earth to the stars."

Seneca

"The part of life we really live is short."

Seneca

"The best revenge is to be unlike him who performed the injury."

Marcus Aurelius

"When you arise in the morning, think of what a precious privilege it is to be alive—to breathe, to think, to enjoy, to love."

Marcus Aurelius

"Your task is to stand straight; not held straight."

Marcus Aurelius

"Death smiles at us all, but all a man can do is smile back."

Marcus Aurelius

"You could leave life right now. Let that determine what you do and say and think."

Marcus Aurelius

"He suffers more than necessary, who suffers before it is necessary."

Seneca

"It's not because things are difficult that we dare not venture. It's because we dare not venture that they are difficult."

Seneca

"The key is to keep company only with people who uplift you, whose presence calls forth your best."

Epictetus

"Don't just say you have read books. Show that through them you have learned to think better, to be a more discriminating and reflective person."

Epictetus

"Any person capable of angering you becomes your master; he can anger you only when you permit yourself to be disturbed by him."

Epictetus

"The good or ill of a man lies within his own will."

Epictetus

"There is no genius without a touch of madness."

Seneca

"Disease is an impediment to the body, but not to the will, unless the will itself chooses. Lameness is an impediment to the leg, but not to the will."

Epictetus

"One of the most beautiful qualities of true friendship is to understand and to be understood."

Seneca

"If you really want to escape the things that harass you, what you're needing is not to be in a different place but to be a different person."

Seneca

"Frequently consider the connection of all things in the universe."

Marcus Aurelius

"How much more grievous are the consequences of anger than the causes of it."

Marcus Aurelius

"You are not your body and hair-style, but your capacity for choosing well. If your choices are beautiful, so too will you be."

Epictetus

"The mind unlearns with difficulty what it has long learned."

Seneca

"Choose not to be harmed — and you won't feel harmed. Don't feel harmed — and you haven't been."

Marcus Aurelius

"The only wealth which you will keep forever is the wealth you have given away."

Marcus Aurelius

"Receive wealth or prosperity without arrogance; and be ready to let it go."

Marcus Aurelius

"Very little is needed for everything to be upset and ruined, only a slight lapse in reason."

Epictetus

"He is a wise man who does not grieve for the things which he has not, but rejoices for those which he has."

Epictetus

"Let philosophy scrape off your own faults, rather than be a way to rail against the faults of others."

Seneca

"Time discovers truth."

Seneca

"The willing are led by fate, the reluctant dragged."

Cleanthes

"First say to yourself what you would be; and then do what you have to do."

Epictetus

"Difficulties strengthen the mind, as labor does the body."

Seneca

"It does not matter what you bear, but how you bear it."

Seneca

"It is not the man who has too little, but the man who craves more, that is poor."

Seneca

"We should not, like sheep, follow the herd of creatures in front of us, making our way where others go, not where we ought to go."

Seneca

"To the wise, life is a problem; to the fool, a solution."

Marcus Aurelius

"To live according to nature is to live according to reason, and to do only those things which the common law of mankind prescribes."

Chrysippus

Conclusion

In the vast tapestry of human existence, Stoicism stands as a beacon of wisdom, guiding individuals through the turbulent seas of life. As we've journeyed together through the pages of this book, we've discovered the profound insights of Stoicism, which have withstood the test of time, proving their universality and relevance to our modern world.

From the introductory overview to the detailed examination of Stoic principles, we've glimpsed into the minds of the great Stoics - individuals who grappled with the very same challenges we face today. Their wisdom reminds us that despite our external circumstances, we hold the ultimate power over our internal world, our perceptions, and our responses.

The Dichotomy of Control elucidated the serenity that comes from discerning between what we can and cannot influence. The Pursuit of Virtue illuminated the Stoic's path to a fulfilled life, underscoring the importance of moral integrity. Chapters on the Inner Fortress and Detachment reinforced the value of cultivating an unassailable mind and spirit, insulating oneself from the vicissitudes of fate.

Stoicism doesn't ask us to dismiss our emotions, but rather, to understand and harness them. Our explorations of Emotions and Desires offered tools for navigating the depths of human feelings, ensuring they serve, rather than enslave us. Coupled with the call for Endurance of Hardship, Stoicism champions resilience and mental fortitude.

Reflection and Continuous Learning emphasized the importance of introspection and the lifelong commitment to knowledge. This is juxtaposed beautifully with the Stoic reflections on Death and Impermanence, teaching us to live with urgency, gratitude, and humility.

At the heart of Stoicism lies the concept of the Universal Reason, or Logos. This principle invites us to see ourselves as part of a grander design, interconnected and interdependent. The Stoic's Cosmopolitanism further amplifies this, advocating for universal kinship and brotherhood.

As we culminated our journey with a collection of Stoic Quotes, we were reminded of the timeless wisdom encapsulated in succinct, potent words, passed down through millennia.

In today's fast-paced, tumultuous world, the teachings of Stoicism offer a refuge. By internalizing and practicing these principles, we can lead lives of greater purpose, tranquility, and fulfillment. Let this book not be an end, but a beginning — a stepping stone in your journey towards mastering the art of Stoic living.

May the wisdom of the Stoics guide you, challenge you, and inspire you to live with authenticity, resilience, and virtue. Embrace the Stoic way of life, and in doing so, discover the profound depths of your own potential.

Printed in Great Britain
by Amazon